GALATIANS

STUDY AID AND COMMENTARY

PASTOR NATHAN A. HOOD

PRESS

Dedication

This book is dedicated to:

The one who continues to amaze me with the revelation knowledge of God's Word; the one who continues to teach me all things and brings the teaching of Christ to my memory; the one who is my greatest Comforter, Counselor, Helper, Intercessor, Advocate, Strengthener and Standby; the one who will remain with me forever; the one to whom I am overwhelmingly honored to dedicate this book; the one who is known as the Holy Spirit.

– Pastor Nathan A. Hood

Acknowledgment

I want to express my love and appreciation for my loving wife, Marilyn. Her continued encouragement, advice, support, and help is the wind beneath my wings. Thank you for believing in me and standing not just behind me, but along side me.

You're the best!

Table of Contents

Chapter 6

Preface

As far as I can remember, I always had a desire to read God's Word; however I didn't always know how to study God's Word. As a Christian I've always known that Christians should read and study the Word of God, the Holy Bible. I often heard ministers say, "Study to show thyself approved..." (II Timothy 2:15), but they never taught nor demonstrated *how* to study the Bible. As a result, I was left on my own and was soon disappointed in trying to study and understand the Holy Bible. In Addition, I've heard some people say that you can't understand the Holy Bible. Even though this appeared to be true, deep down in my heart I knew that it wasn't. Nevertheless, I still had a hunger for understanding God's Word.

As I matured, I understood more; and as I read, God's Spirit began to reveal His Word to me. I gained revelation knowledge when I became more serious in my study of His Word. In addition, I was led to a church where the minister would explain and teach in the Sunday morning worship service. Most of the ministers I heard would preach about God's Word but really didn't teach or explain it. As I gained revelation knowledge from studying the Word of God, I often thought that the revelation I had gained should be written down. That way, the revelation knowledge is not dependent upon human memory. So, I began to write. Initially, I wrote for my personal use. Now, others may be interested in these writings. My goal was very simple: to catalogue my notes and the revealed knowledge that the grace of God has allowed and provided to me.

The numbers such as v. 12 or vv. 19-22, located to the left-hand side of each chapter, represent the verses being discussed. Words that have been deemed noteworthy are followed by their definition in parenthesis. The format of the definition starts with the number that is keyed to Strong's Greek Dictionary of the New Testament (copyright, 1890, by James Strong, Madison, N. J.), followed by a colon (:). Next, the exact equivalent of the Greek word in English letters according to the system of transliteration, followed by a colon. What follows is the precise pronunciation (*italicized*), according to the usual English mode of sounding syllables, also followed by a colon. The **bold type** that follows is the definition of the Greek word in its context. Additionally, there is a blank page at the end of each chapter for your own personal notes. This study is intended as an aid for the serious student of the Holy Bible. Use the study alongside your Bible reading.

To God be the glory!

In His Service,
Nathan A. Hood
Pastor / Teacher

Notes

The name Galatia derived from the people called Galatians (Galatai), which was a Greek modification of their original name, Keltoi or Keltai – a Celtic tribe from ancient Gaul. After having invaded Macedonia and Greece around 280 B.C., they crossed into Asia Minor on the invitation of Nikomedes I, King of Bithynia, to aid him in a civil war. After ravaging far and wide, they were finally confined to northern/central Asia Minor, where they settled as conquerors and gave their name to the territory.

Paul's epistle to the Galatians, probably written between 55 and 60 A.D., has been described as "The Magna Carta of Spiritual Emancipation." Magna Carta is a document that serves as a guarantee of basic rights and it remains as the abiding monument of the liberation of Christianity from the trammels of legalism.

This epistle was a formal written letter to all the assemblies (churches) that Paul planted in Galatia. These assemblies began well. However, Judaizing teachers insisted that unless Gentile Believers were circumcised and obeyed the ceremony of the Mosaic law, they could not be saved. Some Judaizers were Jews who professed to be Christians and some acknowledged Jesus as Messiah. It appears the Judaizers had great success in promulgating their doctrine and leading the Galatian Christians from the simplicity of the gospel. Paul realized that the mixing of the Mosaic law and "grace through faith," neutralized the truth of salvation and would do away with the message of justification by faith in Jesus Christ. To correct this error, Paul wrote this epistle.

This attitude or spirit of the Judaizers has plagued humankind from the beginning and is alive today. The Judaizers attitude can be traced all the way back to Cain and Abel in the book of Genesis. A more contemporary name for this doctrine is "salvation by works." God has already produced His plan for humankind and given His directives. This plan of God is the salvation of humankind and it is a free gift. However, some groups want to do their own plan or add to God's plan. They want God to accept their plan or their additives to His plan. The plan of these groups involves salvation by works and usually brings rules, regulations, traditionalism, and restrictions, which thwart and frustrate the liberty of the gospel (Christianity) and brings people into bondage and control. History is replete with man's attempt to reach up toward God and earn justification through works, when, at the same time, God has already reached down toward humankind, freely giving justification without works. Man needs only to accept God's plan and directives and keep his own ideas out of the way of God's plan, purposes, and directives.

Most churches accept the doctrine of "justification by faith" in Jesus Christ. However, many – usually churches that have a propensity toward traditionalism – have taken the legalism, traditions, and rituals out of the requirements for salvation and applied these same legalistic principles to govern their church. They can be so strict that they still choke their church members and produce bondage in their members. They vote on everything (no matter how insignificant) and can't make a move without consulting by-laws, traditions, and regulations. The pastor is bound and the people are bound by their rules and regulations. Now, rules are a necessity and we must have them, otherwise we'll have chaos in the churches. However, such churches elevate their rules above the law of love and follow the letter of legalistic principles rather than the Spirit, and the law of love takes a back seat to their legalistic practices and traditionalisms. It is in my opinion that fear, control, and the desires for power are usually the motives for such.

CHAPTER 1

Introduction and Salutation

v. 1   Paul (3972:Paulos:*pow'-los*) was an apostle (652:apostolos:*ap-os'-tol-os*:**one sent forth**). His position of being an apostle did not come from man. In other words, neither man nor any type of establishment, government, or learning institution appointed him. He did not receive his apostolic position *through* man; he received it directly through Jesus Christ and God the Father.

v. 2   Paul wrote this epistle from Rome to the churches of Galatia. According to references, Galatia was a district in north-central Asia Minor, the exact boundaries of which are uncertain. The people that inhabited Galatia belonged to the race known as Gauls and immigrated there, about 280 B.C., after crossing over from Thrace.

v. 3   Grace   (5485:charis:*khar'-ece*:**favor**). Paul's customary greeting was to desire the granting of God's and our Lord Jesus Christ's favor and peace upon the person or group that was receiving his greeting. This greeting also testifies to the deity of Jesus Christ.

v. 4   Jesus Christ gave Himself and endured the crucifixion on the cross for the *sin nature*, not the sins, of humankind. It is our sin nature that causes us to perform acts of sin. Jesus Christ gave His body and blood (a physical sacrifice) to redeem humankind back into a position of being in a right standing relationship with God, our Father. By giving Himself, He delivered us from the result, culmination, and zenith of this present evil wicked age. It was the will of God, our Father, that we be delivered.

Note: The word *world* in the King James Version is more accurately translated *age* (165:aion: *ahee-ohn'*: **a period of indefinite duration. Not so much the length of a period, but a period marked by spiritual or moral characteristics**).

In other words, it was the objective and purpose of Jesus Christ, by giving Himself to die, to deliver us from this present evil age – and the daily trials that we experience in this present evil age – by lifting us above these present trials and giving us citizenship in the kingdom of God. We don't deny that we feel the affect or influence of the trials of this present evil age. However, because we have citizenship in the kingdom of God, we believe and have faith that we'll not experience the results, culmination, and zenith of the present trials of this present evil age because they are beneath us; we've been lifted above them. We don't magnify the trials of this present evil age with our words. Instead, we magnify the solution and the positive end result with our words. We have been delivered; therefore we'll rise above it and not succumb to it because of our faith in what God our Father did for us in and through Jesus Christ.

Now that we *have been* (past tense) delivered from this present evil age and the daily trials that we experience in this present evil age, the question is how do we access this deliverance? We access our deliverance by exercising our *faith*. In other words, since we believe that we have been delivered from this present evil age, our words and actions are to be in agreement with what we believe. When the trials of this evil age begin to try to manifest in our lives, we resist those trials with our words and actions. We base our words and actions on what God's Word says, "...that He might deliver us from this present evil age." Therefore, our whole mindset and attitude is set toward having been delivered from the present trials. In the midst of the trials, we're focused on the deliverance or solution. And while in the trials, we thank God and praise Him with joy in our hearts and with an attitude of excitement, expectancy, and enthusiasm for the deliverance and solution has already been provided and will manifest shortly. What gives us this attitude is our faith in His Word – that He will perform what He said.

v. 5   The word *glory* means the physical manifestation of the power of God.

Paul's Astonishment Towards the Galatians' Departure from the True Gospel

vv. 6-7   Paul was astonished when he had received word that the churches in Galatia had so soon deviated from the gospel (2098:euaggelion:*yoo-ang-ghel'-ee-on*:**the good news or good tidings of the kingdom of God**) that he preached to them when he was with them. Others (Judaizers) had come into the Galatian churches and began to add to or replace the teachings of Paul that were of Christ. Apparently, the Galatians recognized these Judaizers as having some type of authority; why else would they have listened to them? Though the Judaizers may have been honest and sincere in their teaching, it is possible to still error. It is believed that some, not all, Judaizers professed to be Christians, accepting Jesus Christ as Messiah. However, they error in their teaching, desiring man to continue to observe the teaching of the Mosaic law.

I believe these Galatian Christians were excited about their new faith in Jesus Christ and were zealous to follow Christ's teachings that they had received from Paul. These Judaizers perverted (3344:meta-strepho:*met-as-tref'-o*:**to transform into something of an opposite character**) the gospel of

Christ and persuaded these Galatian Christians to observe their teachings. It is apparent also that these Galatian Christians did not have such writings as we Christians have today. Otherwise they would have consulted New Testament Scriptures and compared them to the teachings of the Judaizers. There will always be ministers that will come to us via the pulpit, books, television and other media. The message here is to *make sure all teachings line up with the gospel of Christ.* Or else we too can be taken away from the gospel of Christ.

vv. 8-9   Paul went on further to admonish (admonish – *to reprove mildly or kindly, but seriously*) the Galatian Christians not to accept any other gospel than what he preached to them, regardless of whether it's a man or a supernatural manifestation such as an angel (32:aggelos:*ang'-el*-os: **a messenger sent by God, man or Satan**) from heaven. By making this statement, Paul was confident in the unity of the Godhead that there are no contradictions in God, the Son, and the Holy Spirit. Anything that is contrary to the gospel of Christ is not of God. Paul instructed that any individual who comes preaching a different gospel other than what he had preached to the Galatian churches, let that individual be cursed (331:anathema:*an-ath'-em-ah*:**excommunicated; the disfavor of Jehovah; devoted to destruction, doomed to eternal punishment**). Paul makes a very strong statement here. It shows how sincere and serious the consequences will be to anyone that preaches a different gospel to God's people. It is clear that preaching a gospel other than the gospel of Jesus Christ carries severe penalties.

Paul's Defense and Proclamation of His Character

v. 10   In this verse, Paul, defends and proclaims the integrity of his own character by asking the Galatian Christians the question of pleasing God or man. I believe he is causing them to remember their encounter with him in the beginning. He asks them does he seek to persuade (3982:peitho: *pi'-tho*:**to apply persuasion, to prevail upon or win over, to persuade, bringing about a change of mind by the influence of reason or moral considerations**) man or God? He states that if he seeks to please people, then he has no place in being a minister (apostle) of Christ. What we can glean from this is that ministers (as well as the laity) – when it comes to the truth of the gospel of Christ and our own personal integrity and character – should not seek the popularity and acceptance of people over and above the truth of the gospel of Christ as well as our own Christian personal ethics and morality. In doing so, we will more than likely compromise the gospel of Christ and our own ethical and moral character.

Paul's Further Defense of the Genuineness of the Gospel of Jesus Christ

v. 11   Certify   (1107:gnorizo:*gno-rid'-zo*:**to   make known; declare, give to understand**). Paul wants the Galatian churches to understand that the gospel that he preached to them did not have its origin in humankind. It is not man's gospel, (A.V. *"a human invention, according to or patterned after any human standard."*).

v. 12   Paul went on to say that he didn't learn about the gospel in a man-made institution of learning. Paul states that the gospel of Christ came to him through a direct revelation given by Jesus Christ Himself. This is the strongest accreditation a Christian can receive. God, through the Holy Spirit, still uses the medium of revelation to impart knowledge to people today.

vv. 13-14   Conversation   (391:anastrophe:*an-as-trof-ay'*: **behavior; manner of life**). In these two verses, Paul continues to defend the genuineness of the gospel of Christ. He reminds the Galatian Christians, concerning his background, how he persecuted (1377:dioko:*dee-o'-ko*:**to   put   to   flight,   drive away; press toward**) the church of God and wasted (4199:portheo:*por-theh'-o*:**to   ravage,   destroy, waste**) it beyond measure. This shows how zealous and sincere Paul was. He believed that he was right in persecuting the church of Christ. This also shows how passionate he was in following the teachings and traditions (legalism and ceremonialism) of his forefathers. It is possible that his passion made him a prime candidate to be used by God.

Note: It is interesting to note that God allowed Paul to persecute the church in its young state. I don't believe it was God's perfect will for Paul (then named Saul) to persecute the church. However, I'm sure there were Christians praying that God intervene and stop this persecution of the Christians.

Paul continues his defense and explains that he profited (4298:prokopto:*prok-op'-to*:**to drive forward, advance; to grow, increase**) in his religion above his peers because he was more zealous toward the traditions of his forefathers. Remember, Paul is defending the gospel of Christ. Why would he say this? I believe he is telling the Galatian Christians that since he was profiting where he was (he gained the respect of his peers and was doing well in the Jewish religion), why would he change unless the gospel of Christ was genuine? Why would he give up all that he had gained and that took years to get in the Jewish religion unless Christ's gospel was the truth? Paul was convinced that Jesus Christ is the Messiah.

vv. 15-24   Continuing his defense, Paul says that despite what he had done in his past it still pleased (2106: eudokeo:*yoo-dok-eh'*:**to be well pleased, think it good; not merely an understanding of what is right and good, but stressing the willingness and freedom of an intention or resolve**

regarding what is good) God to call him, reveal Jesus Christ the Messiah to him, and equip him to preach the gospel to the Gentiles (the non-Jewish world). God's calling of Paul to preach the gospel of Christ is an expression of God's grace (unearned favor) toward Paul. Paul did not deserve this calling of God by merit or deeds. Paul didn't earn this calling of God because of his deeds and accomplishments. God expressed His sovereignty and chose Paul. This shows us that God does not think like we think. If man was to choose someone for Paul's task, we would not have chosen Paul. We would have chosen someone that was already in our camp; the best man for the job by human standards such as resumes, outward appearances, social status, and charisma.

Paul is reaffirming to the Galatian Christians that the gospel that he preached is not from man. He states that when God called him to preach the gospel of Christ to the Gentiles, he didn't go running to man (flesh and blood). He didn't seek the counsel of teachers or professors. He didn't go to man's institutions of higher learning. He states that he didn't even try to go to Jerusalem and learn from those that were apostles before he was an apostle. Instead, he went into Arabia, a country south of Damascus. Here, Paul seems to have received his theological course of study from Jesus Christ Himself. After spending some time in Arabia, he returned to Damascus. Paul is telling this to the Galatian Christians so they can compare the gospel he proclaimed to them that came from

God alone and what the Judaizers taught that was contrary to the gospel he preached.

Paul further states that he went to Jerusalem three years after he had returned to Damascus from Arabia. He stayed with Peter (Cephas) fifteen days and met only one other apostles, James, the Lord's brother. Paul continues to reaffirm that the gospel that he preached did not come from man. He even said that he is telling the truth before God.

Paul states that after he left Jerusalem, he went to the regions of Syria and Cilicia. The Christians there didn't even know his face and weren't capable of recognizing who he was. They didn't even know who he was, so he couldn't have conferred and counseled with them because they didn't even know him. They glorified God because they heard that the one that used to persecute the church of Christ in time past, now preaches the gospel of Christ.

Summary and Conclusion

Because of the abundance of evidence that Paul presents in this chapter, we can *honestly* conclude that Paul received his revelation of the gospel of Christ from Christ Himself and not from humankind, and that the Judaizers' teachings were contrary to the plan and purpose of God's salvation plan of justification by faith in Jesus Christ. Amen!

Personal Notes

CHAPTER 2

Paul's Teachings Accepted by the Repute of Jerusalem

vv. 1-2   Here, Paul continues to defend his teachings of
the gospel of Jesus Christ vs. the false teachings of
the Judaizers. After Paul visited Syria and Cilicia
(chapter 1:21), fourteen years passed before he went
back to Jerusalem, and this time he had Barnabas
and Titus with him. Paul is continuing to show that
he didn't confer with people to obtain his teachings
of the gospel of Christ. This visit to Jerusalem was
special and by divine revelation. Paul communi-
cated to the Jews of Jerusalem the same gospel that
he preached to the Gentiles. However, he reported
his teachings privately to the repute (1380:dokeo:
dok-eh'-o:**well thought of; which were of reputation**) of Jerusalem to avoid an uprising among
the mass of Christians in Jerusalem. He didn't want
those without an open mind to misunderstand his
teachings and his work. This shows wisdom on the
part of Paul. His goal was to be heard and by going

in privately to the repute of Jerusalem, they had an opportunity to hear him.

A lesson to be learned here is that sometimes we must use non-conventional methods to minister to the lost. We must be very careful that the message doesn't get lost in the packaging of the message. For example, many Christians have put the message of the gospel of Jesus Christ to music. Some people put more emphasis on the music and celebrate the sound of music carrying a beat that they like, rather than listening to the words of the music. You can't hear the message if you're focused only on the sounds of the music. We must be careful not to let the message take a back seat to a popular sound. We often celebrate the artist or performer rather than the gospel message itself.

vv. 3-5   While Paul attended this private counsel meeting with the repute of Jerusalem – quite possibly a conference meeting with the apostles and elders – it is likely that Barnabas and Titus were in attendance. Paul gave them the same gospel that he gave the Gentiles. Being a Greek, Titus was not circumcised. The counsel didn't require or urge him to be circumcised, even though Titus was a preacher. In other words, those who were of a good reputation accepted and agreed with Paul's teachings of the gospel of Jesus Christ. This was like a "slap in the face" to the Judaizing teachers. This decision regarding Titus was a condemnation toward the Judaizers.

Paul's concern was that these false teachers were secretly brought into the body of Christ to spy out the liberty of Christianity, which is void of the legalism and ceremonialism of the Law. The end result of these false teachers was to bring these Galatian Christians into bondage under the law of Moses. As I stated before, it seems that man has a propensity to bring people into bondage and control with rules, regulations, and restrictions. Paul, and those that were with him, did not submit to these false teachers, not even once, so that the truth of the gospel of Christ may continue without compromise.

vv. 6-10   Paul says that the repute of Jerusalem made no new requirements of him nor did they make any suggestions. Additionally, their status did not influence him because God does not show partiality or recognize external distinctions of people.

What we can learn from this is that we do not need to seek man's permission, approval, or disapproval concerning God's directives before we can follow His plan and purpose. We get our "marching orders" from Jesus Christ and man's approval or permission is irrelevant to God's directive, unless God directs us by revelation as He did in this case with Paul.

Instead of the repute of Jerusalem coming down on Paul and correcting his teachings of the gospel of Jesus Christ (which the Judaizers would have loved), they did the opposite. When they saw that Paul had been entrusted to preach the gospel of Christ to the Gentiles (the uncircumcised) as Peter had been entrusted to preach the gospel of Christ to the Jews (the circumcised), they agreed. The

God that motivated, equipped, and worked through Peter for the mission to the Jews (the circumcised), was the same God that motivated, equipped, and worked through Paul for the mission to the Gentiles (the uncircumcised). When James, the brother of Jesus, Cephas (Peter) and John, who were pillars in the church body, perceived the unmerited favor that God had extended to Paul, they gave Paul and Barnabas the right hand of fellowship. They asked only that they remember the poor, which they did anyway. This action, I'm sure, was very disappointing to the false teachers (the Judaizers), and I believe it fueled their anger toward Paul.

Note: It is interesting that James, Peter, and John told Paul and Barnabas to remember the poor. Poor people don't say to other poor people to remember the poor. This implies that they were not poor. Tradition has painted them poor, but a careful study of the Scriptures shows that they were not poor people. Why would they say to Paul and Barnabas to remember the poor and they were poor themselves? If James, Peter, and John were poor, wouldn't they say instead to Paul and Barnabas to remember *us* poor people? I submit here that they weren't poor people.

Paul Confronts Peter's Instability and explains to the Galatian Christians

vv. 11-16   Paul begins to deal with an issue that had to do with Peter's actions. It is very possible that the Galatian Christians had heard what Peter was doing and more than likely the Judaizers were using Peter's actions to support their teachings to the Galatian Christians. Therefore, I believe that Paul felt it was necessary to confront this issue.

Peter's actions were wrong and when Paul caught up with him in the city of Antioch, he protested and opposed Peter to his face, in front of everyone, concerning his conduct. It was custom for Jews not to eat meals with Gentiles. When the people from Jerusalem (from James) arrived, Peter withdrew himself from the Gentiles out of fear, and ate only with the Jews from Jerusalem. This showed instability, pretense, prejudice, and hypocrisy on Peter's part. This circumstance did not create Peter's instability, pretense, prejudice, and hypocrisy; it revealed what was already inside him.

Note: Peter displayed this same character trait when the Roman soldiers took Jesus captive. He denied Jesus three times (Matthew 26:69-75). When confronted with truth and the pressure of what's popular with society, Peter had a weakness to compromise the truth and go along with the majority of society in order to avoid repercussions. Here, Peter had an opportunity to be strong, but his instability over-powered is judgment.

Not only was Peter guilty of concealing his true convictions, but the Jews that were with Peter were also guilty insomuch that even Barnabas was also carried away with their dissimulation (5272:hupokrisis:*hoop-ok'-ree-sis*:**acting under a feigned [feign** – *to give a false appearance, not real, pretend*] **part; deceit**). I believe that such circumstances give us opportunity to: 1) take note of our thoughts, responses, and actions; 2) compare what's going on deep in our hearts, words, and actions to what is right and wrong in the eyes of Christ; and finally, 3) learn from our mistakes and make corrections so that we don't repeat the error of our ways. By doing this, we continue to grow and mature in our walk with Christ.

Therefore, when Paul saw that Peter wasn't straightforward and wasn't living up to the truth of the gospel of Jesus Christ, he publicly "read the riot act" (*figure of speech*) to Peter. Remember, Paul is communicating to the Galatian Christians.

Paul explains to the Galatian Christians what he said to Peter and everyone present. He asked Peter a very pointed question: If Peter, born a Jew, can live like the Gentiles – free from the rituals and ceremonialism of Judaism, why then does he now urge (practically force) the Gentiles to comply with the rituals and ceremonialism of Judaism? This went to the heart of the issue and Peter couldn't defend it. Paul went on to say that even though both Peter and himself are Jews by birth and not

Gentile sinners, knowing that man is not justified or declared righteous by keeping, doing, and living by the works of the Law, but only through faith and absolute reliance on, adherence to and trust in Jesus Christ the Messiah.

Paul said that even we (Peter and Paul) have accepted and believe on Jesus Christ that we might be justified by faith in Jesus Christ and not justified by the deed and words of the Law. Humankind cannot be justified by observing any rituals of the Law given by Moses, because by observing and doing these rituals and traditions of the Law, no human can ever be justified (declared righteous; to be in right standing with God). See Galatians 3:11, Ephesians 2:8-9, Titus 3:5, and Romans 3:20. This is why Paul's writings to the Galatian Christians have been described as "The Magna Carta of Spiritual Emancipation" and it remains as the abiding monument of the liberation of Christianity from the trammels (*restrictions*) of legalism.

vv. 17-18   In addition, Paul said to Peter that they themselves seek to be declared righteous (right standing with God) solely through faith in Jesus Christ, and not by the keeping of the law of Moses. By accepting justification by faith in Jesus Christ, they admit they're sinners and are convicted of sin, just like the Gentiles.

Paul asked Peter, "...Is therefore Christ the minister of sin?" Paul was really asking: *Has Christ provided a gospel that does not deal effectually with sin? Are those who are justified by faith in Him still sinners or partially justified, so that they must go back to the Law for total and complete justification and cleansing?* God forbid! Paul says he would be a transgressor if he forsakes Christ's work on the cross by adhering to the Law, which he has worked all these years to tear down, destroy and do away with.

vv. 19-21   Paul states that as far as the Law is concerned, he is now dead to it. Gentiles never practiced the law of Moses because it was never given to them. Gentiles didn't seek justification through the Law. However, the Jews had the law of Moses and now that Christ the Messiah has come and fulfilled the Law, they are now dead to it. Both Jews and Gentiles receive justification in and through Jesus Christ. We both live unto God through Jesus Christ and keep the law of love, not the law of Moses, because Christ fulfilled the Law.

Now, we have been crucified with Christ. When Christ was crucified, God saw us crucified, spiritually. What this means is that we don't live unto ourselves, by our own rules. We have taken on the nature of Christ, the kingdom of God, and we choose to follow our new nature. The Holy Spirit resides in us as Christ's representative. We're *born* of the Holy Spirit, but not *filled* with the Holy Spirit. Being *born* of the Spirit and being *filled* with the Spirit are two different functions or experiences.

The Spirit of God dwells in us as the Spirit of Christ (Romans 8:9). The Spirit of Christ dwells in our hearts *by faith* (Ephesians 3:17). The Spirit of Christ begins to live His life through us according and subject to our choice and will. We follow God's love law. It is no longer I who lives, but the Spirit of Christ that is in me lives. The life that we now live in this body we live or have spiritual life by faith in Jesus Christ; and not by doing the deeds of the law of Moses. Therefore, we're not to treat this gift from God as something of minor importance. We're not to frustrate (114:atheteo:*ath-et-eh'-o*:**to set aside, to disesteem, neutralize or violate; to make void**) this unmerited favor that God has given us through Jesus Christ. It is not something to be trivialized or even tampered with because if righteousness, justification, and being in right standing with God could come through the keeping of the law of Moses (observing the rituals and legalisms of the Law), then Christ died on the cross for nothing and all His work was in vain.

Summary and Conclusion

We're justified (declared righteous; in right standing with God), not by observing and doing the rituals and legalistic practices of the Law of Moses, but by *faith alone* in the work that Jesus did on the cross – the shedding of His blood on our behalf.

Personal Notes

CHAPTER 3

Receiving the Holy Spirit by the Works of the Law or by the Hearing of Faith?

vv. 1-5   Paul seems to vent some frustration here by saying that they are foolish (453:anoetos:*an-o'-ay-tos*:**unintelligent, unwise; signifies not understanding, an unworthy lack of understanding, senseless**).

>   Note: This word "foolish", in the original text, is a different word than used in Matt. 5:22.

Paul taught these Galatian Christians that accepting Christ crucified is the only means and grounds for salvation – minus keeping the legalistic practices of the law of Moses. Paul knew they knew this, so, at first, he was astonished, but his astonishment seems to have grown into frustration. He wondered how they could possibly turn from the truth. Paul asked them who put a spell on them or fascinated them or bewitched (940:baskaino:

bas-kah'-ee-no:**fascinate by false representation; to mislead by an evil eye, and so to charm; leading into evil doctrine**) them to cause them to turn from the truth, when they knew that Jesus Christ the Messiah was portrayed as crucified?

Paul asked them another very pointed and comparative question: Did they receive the Holy Spirit by obeying the Law and doing its works or by hearing the message of the gospel of Christ and believing it? If they were honest, they'd have to admit their error. Here is a revelation in Paul's question: *You cannot receive the Holy Spirit by keeping the legalistic practices of the law of Moses.* Christians cannot receive the Holy Spirit by doing works. We receive the Holy Spirit by hearing the gospel of Jesus Christ and accepting Him by faith. Salvation comes by faith alone, not emotions. Many times Christians use their emotions and feelings to gauge their faith. This is one of the biggest errors we Christians can make. Faith has nothing to do with feelings and emotions. Christians who rely on feelings and emotions as a guide to their spiritual development struggle and find it difficult to mature beyond a "puppy love" stage. This phenomenon is usually due to a lack of teaching and knowledge.

The Galatian Christians began their spiritual walk relying upon the Holy Spirit, but when they listened to the Judaizers, they added the keeping of the law of Moses as a requirement for their salvation. They came to believe that Jesus' work on the cross was insufficient to complete their salvation, and they foolishly believed not only were they to accept Jesus' work on the cross, but in addition, they must also keep the law of Moses to move them into perfection or maturity. Paul asked them if they were really that foolish.

Evidently, the Galatian Christians had endured some type of opposition to their profession of faith in Jesus Christ. Paul asked had they suffered (3958:pascho:*pas'-kho*:**to experience a sensation or impression, usually painful**) for nothing and now going to throw it all away?

In continuing to question the Galatian Christians, it seems that Paul's motive is to cause them to think about what they were doing. God had given His precious Holy Spirit to these Galatian Christians and, through Paul's ministry, worked many wonderful miracles (1411:dunamis:*doo'-nam-is*:**power, inherent ability; works of a supernatural origin and character such as could not be produced by natural agents and means**) among them. Paul simply asked had these things been done due to their keeping and doing the legalistic practices of the law of Moses or by hearing, accepting, and receiving by faith the gospel of Jesus Christ? Salvation came by faith and the working of miracles came by faith also. God confirmed the gospel of Jesus Christ to be true by working miracles through His minister among the people. The miracles were saying "yes" and "amen" to the gospel of Jesus Christ. The miracles confirmed the gospel of Jesus Christ, the Word!

Justification by Faith or by the Works of the Law?

vv. 6-9   Paul further supports his position by explaining that Abraham simply believed what God promised him, and because of his faith and belief, Abraham was justified in God's eyes. God justified Abraham and declared him righteous because he believed and had faith in God's Word and promises to him (Romans 4:17-21), not by keeping and doing legalistic works. The true children or descendents of Abraham are not those who keep the law of Moses, but those who accept the gospel of Jesus Christ by faith and belief. This means that Gentiles who believe are also declared righteous (justified by God through faith in Jesus Christ) and are included as the children of Abraham – his spiritual descendents. Paul further explains that God revealed this to Abraham when He said that *all* families of the earth will be blessed (Genesis 12:3). God has promised to justify and declare Gentiles righteous through faith alone, not by keeping the law of Moses. Therefore, Gentile Christians are blessed along with Abraham.

What this also says is that it was God's plan and purpose all along to include the Gentiles in His salvation plan. Again, God told Abraham that *all* families of the earth will be blessed. God never declared humankind righteous by keeping and doing the legalistic practices of the laws of Moses. God's plan was, and still is, that *only* by His grace, through faith in the gospel of Jesus Christ, will He justify humankind and declare humankind righteous.

v. 10 Paul also affirms to the Galatian Christians that those who are seeking and depending on justification by keeping the law of Moses with its ritual practices are operating under the curse (2671:katara: *kat-ar'-ah*:**denotes an execration [execrate – *to inveigh* [inveigh – *to give vent to angry censure; protest with intense emotion or conviction*] *against, denounce*], imprecation [imprecation – *to invoke (evil or a curse) upon*], curse, uttered out of malevolence [malevolence – *ill will toward others; wishing harm to others*]**) of the Law. If one is to operate within the law of Moses without being under the curse, they must continue to practice *all* of the precepts and commands written in the book of the Law (Deuteronomy 27:26). No one, except Jesus, was able to keep the entire Law.

It is interesting to note that the law of Moses was not given to the Gentiles and they could not lay claim to the blessings of Abraham without becoming a proselyte to Judaism. However, receiving salvation through faith in the gospel of Jesus Christ gives Gentiles the position of being children of Abraham and heirs to the promises of Abraham.

v. 11 Here, Paul is very straightforward and says to the Galatian Christians that, based on the evidence, no one is justified in God's eyes by observing and doing the works of the law of Moses. The evidence upon which Paul bases his argument include: 1) the revelation of the gospel of Christ that Paul received (Galatians 1:11-12) and 2) God confirming the gospel of Christ with the working of miracles through Paul's ministry, Galatians 3:5.

It is interesting to note that he said, "… in the sight of God." It is possible to be justified by works in the sight of people. People will justify you as long as you are keeping their traditions, rules, and practices. However, God declares us righteous (right standing with Him) by His grace through faith in the gospel of Jesus Christ. Since the fall of Adam, God has never justified people through ritualistic practices and the legalisms of anyone's law. God has always justified people through faith in the revelation of God (Habakkuk 2:4). Therefore, the just shall live or have spiritual life (2198:zao: *dzah'-o*:**to live, be alive; spiritual life**) by faith in the gospel of Jesus Christ.

vv. 12-14   The law of Moses had nothing to do with faith. If a person is practicing of the law of Moses, then they are living in the Law. However, there is no redemption in the law of Moses. The deeds of the Law are too defective and fall far short of obtaining justification. If there could be justification in keeping the law of Moses, then what do we need Christ for? Those that choose to be under the Law are operating under the curse of the Law.

Christ purchased our freedom and redeemed us from the curse of the Law and its' condemnation. He did this by taking our sin upon Himself and bearing the penalty due us upon His own Person. In doing so, He also became a curse on our behalf. He substituted Himself as our sin. He was our propitiation (conciliatory offering).

The Scriptures say, "… Cursed is every one that hangeth on a tree:" The meaning of this saying is defined in Deuteronomy 21:22-23: When a person commits a crime (sin) that deserves the death penalty (capital punishment) such as the gallows (hanging), that person must be hung on a tree. In today's society, the gas chamber or lethal injection is the penalty. In the Old Testament, God said the person is to be hung on a tree and buried the same day, because the person that is hung is accursed (7045:*qelalah*:**curse, vilification [vilification** *– defame, denigrate*]**, execration [execrate** *– to inveigh* **[inveigh** *– to give vent to angry censure; protest with intense emotion or conviction*] *against, denounce*]) of God and it would otherwise defile the land. Everyone that commits a crime and is sentenced to capital punishment is cursed of God. Jesus was sentenced to capital punishment (crucifixion), and therefore Jesus Christ became cursed. Jesus Christ was accursed so that the Gentiles who received Christ by faith would receive the blessing and promise (justification through faith) of Abraham. In other words, through faith in Jesus Christ, all receive the realization of the promise of the indwelling Holy Spirit as Christ's representative and receive the blessings of Abraham.

God's promise to Abraham was both spiritual and physical/material (see Genesis 12:1-3). Abraham had the human sinful nature and could not experience nor receive the new birth. He could not be born again because Christ the Messiah had not yet come (Romans 10:9-10). God promised Abraham that "... in thee shall *all* families of the earth be blessed." This *spiritual promise* was the indwelling Holy Spirit as Christ's representative for *all* people who receive Jesus Christ the Messiah as their Lord and Savior. Abraham was unable to experience this *spiritual promise* because Christ did not come until about 3,430 years later. Still, God justified Abraham and declared him righteous because he believed and had faith in God's promise to him. Since Abraham was unable to experience this *spiritual promise*, how did God bless Abraham so that he personally could experience the promised blessing? God had to deal with Abraham externally (physically and materially) because Abraham was internally (spiritually) dead, cut off from God. God told him, "... I will make thee a great nation ... I will bless *thee* ... and make thy name great ... I will bless them that bless *thee*." The *blessing* was physical/material and the *promise* was spiritual.

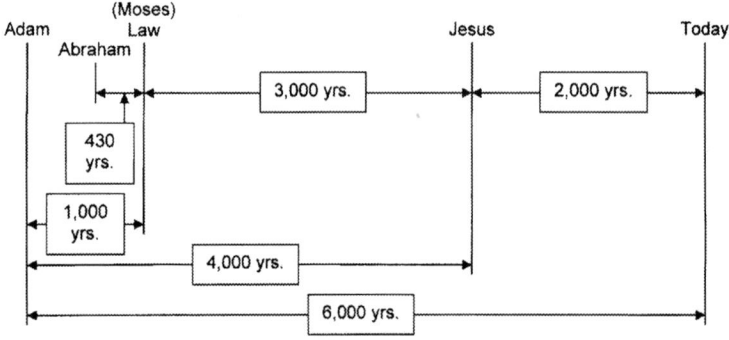

Note: The above time line is an approximation.

vv. 15-18   Here, Paul draws a comparison between God's covenant and a human's covenant. He states to the Galatian Christians that when a person dies, his or her legal will and testament (a mere human covenant) is final because it has been signed and nota-rized (*ratified and confirmed*). A man's covenant will stand up in any court of the land.

Now God decreed the promise to Abraham and his *seed* (singular), not his seeds (plural). This one seed – descendent – is obviously none other than Jesus Christ the Messiah.

So Paul's argument was that the decreed promise of God had its beginning 430 years before the Law was instituted; and the Law cannot set aside the promise of the covenant, or render it void, nor add anything to it. In short, the promise of salvation preceded the giving of the Law by 430 years and the Law cannot disannul (208:akuroo:*ak-oo-ro'-o*:**to invalidate, make of none effect; to make void; to deprive of authority**) the promise of the covenant no more than a signed and notarized (*ratified and confirmed*) last will and testament can be annulled. So Paul was telling the Galatian Christians that the gospel of Jesus Christ that is received by faith cannot be replaced with keeping and doing the legalistic practices and rituals of the law of Moses. If our inheritance of the promise of the covenant comes to us by keeping and doing the law of Moses, which the Judaizers teach, then salvation is no longer by and through Jesus Christ. But God *did* give it to Abraham as a free gift, solely by virtue of His promise, and Abraham received that promise by faith.

The Function and Purpose of the Law of Moses

vv. 19-29   After all that Paul has said to the Galatian Christians, he realized the following question should be addressed: Then what was the purpose of the law of Moses in the first place? Why was it given? The Law was given 430 years after the promise had be given for the following purpose: 1) to expose and disclose people's guilt because of their transgressions (3847:parabasis:*par-ab'-as-is*:**violation, breaking; is used metaphorically to denote transgression [always of a breach of law]**) and to make people more conscience of their sinfulness and 2) to remain in effect *until* the seed (Jesus Christ) comes. The Law came through an intermediary, Moses.

A mediator (go-between or intermediary) implies more than one party. God was one person (party) and was the sole party in giving the promise to Abraham. The Law was a contract between God and Israel, not the Gentiles.

When you look at the law of Moses and the promise of the gospel of Jesus Christ by faith, one might say that they oppose each other. The key to our understanding of this is to know the purpose of the Law and the capacity in which the law of Moses served. If righteousness (being justified and declared righteous by God) could be extended toward humankind through the Law, then there would be no reason for the promise of the gospel of Jesus Christ by faith, because righteousness would have been by the law of Moses. The Law was designed to help lead people to accept the promise of salvation through faith in the gospel of Jesus Christ.

The Scriptures conclude that all people are under sin and are born with the sinful nature; therefore, there is no escape for all people are under the curse of the Law. For this cause was the promise of the gospel of Jesus Christ given to the Believers. Before the promise of the gospel of Jesus Christ came, Israel was kept under the law of Moses until the manifestation of the promise. The law of Moses was basically a tutor, trainer or child-guide for Israel, leading them to the promise of the gospel of Jesus Christ, so, eventually, and in the final analysis, we all (Jews and Gentiles) can be justified by faith in the promise of the gospel of Jesus Christ. Now that the promise of the gospel of Jesus Christ by faith has come, the tutor or child-guide is no longer necessary. We're not under the curse of the Law. Christ redeemed us. The law of Moses was not bad; it has just fulfilled its purpose. This is why going back to the rituals and legalistic practices of the law of Moses is senseless.

Note: Though we do not rely on the Law for salvation, we must remember and acknowledge that *all* Scripture is God-breathed and helpful for teaching correction, guidance, etc. (see, 2 Timothy 3:16, Hebrews 4:12, Luke 11:28). Additionally, the Law tells us how to avoid the mines in the minefields of life, especially the Proverbs, and shows us the error of our ways.

All believers are now children of God by faith in the gospel of Jesus Christ; they are baptized and identified in Christ and clothed with Christ.

Note: The word "baptized" in verse 27 does not refer to water baptism. It refers to being enveloped in the body of Christ. When one accepts Jesus Christ as Lord and Savior, the Holy Spirit envelops them into the body of Christ. Water baptism is not an essential element in salvation. However, Christ commands us to be baptized (immersed) in water upon accepting Jesus Christ as Lord and Savior. Water baptism is an outward sign of an inward grace. It is a sign to the world that a person is identified with Christ.

Now, there is no distinction between Jews or Gentiles (Greek), slave or free, male or female, because we *all* are one in Christ Jesus. Now that we're Christ's, we're all Abraham's seed (by faith, spiritually), heirs of the blessings of Abraham, and the promise of the gospel of Jesus Christ by faith.

Summary and Conclusion

Do we receive the Holy Spirit as a representative of Christ by keeping and doing the rituals and legalistic practices of the law of Moses or by hearing and receiving the gospel of Jesus Christ by faith? Does God confirm with signs, wonders, and miracles the law of Moses or His Word, the gospel of Jesus Christ? We must conclude that we receive salvation by faith in the gospel of Jesus Christ and not by keeping the law of Moses. We're justified – declared the righteousness of God – by His grace through faith in the gospel of Jesus Christ and not by keeping the Law.

Christ has redeemed us from the curse of the Law so that the blessings of Abraham can come upon the Gentiles and the promised Holy Spirit, as a representative of Christ, can be realized and experienced by those who believe and receive the gospel of Jesus Christ by faith.

The purpose of the law of Moses was to enlighten the children of Israel how sinful humankind is and to guide them like a tutor, schoolmaster, or trainer until the promised Messiah comes. Now that the promised Messiah has come, we're no longer under the curse of the Law. There is no more distinction of Jew and Gentile or male and female, we're all one in God's eyes.

Personal Notes

CHAPTER 4

Return to the Bondage of the Law? God Forbid!

vv. 1-7   One might say at this point there is no need for
Paul to continue defending his position given all
the preponderance of information and evidence
he's already presented. But the Holy Spirit has
given him more information to share. Paul paints
another allegoric picture: He compares the children of Israel, who were under the law of Moses,
to that of a child under the discipline, tutelage, and
restraint of its guardians. The child is in this position until the father appoints him to take over the
estate – usually when the minor becomes an adult.
The adult then assumes the responsibilities of his
position and gives directives to the servants of the
house. Israel was under the bondage of the discipline, tutelage, and restraint of the law of Moses.
When the fullness of time had come as determined
by Father God, He sent His Son, Jesus Christ (born
of a woman and also subject to the law of Moses)
to purchase our freedom and redeem us from the

law of Moses so that we might be adopted as sons and no longer servants. In other words, Believers passed from the position of servitude into the liberty of sonship in Christ. We're now sons of God and not just servants (1401:doulos:*doo'-los*: **frequently indicating subjection without the idea of bondage; used metaphorically of spiritual, moral and ethical conditions**) of God. The servant has a fellowship with the father. But the actual child (now an adult) has, not just a closer fellowship, but also a relationship with the father and more liberty and privilege than the servant. The father and child have a special parent-child relationship.

Because of Jesus, we're sons and daughters of God! The children of Israel were servants of God, not sons. The Israelites didn't enjoy the fellowship and relationship with the Father that we have today. God has placed His precious Holy Spirit, as a representative of Christ, in His children's spirit. Hence, Believers have the Spirit of Christ. Because of Jesus, children of God can call God, "Father" and they are heirs of God through Jesus Christ.

Note: Though the children of Israel were servants of God, they were His chosen people; "my people," "the Branch of the Lord," "the Vineyard of the Lord Almighty" and David's writings in the Psalms dripped with love and adoration to the Lord.

vv. 8 – 12   Paul now reminds the Galatian Christians of their past. Before they came into the knowledge of the gospel of Jesus Christ, they were in bondage to idols; gods that didn't exist.

Note: Even the religion of idols produced bondage in their followers. Idols don't create their own religious practices because the gods don't exist. People such as the high priest or prophet create the religious practices of idols. They produce rules, regulations, and religious practices for followers to obey. The end result is bondage and control over people. Christianity sets us free from such bondage. Jesus said, "... For my yoke *is easy* and my burden is light" (Matthew 11:30).

Now that the Galatian Christians have come into the knowledge of the gospel of Jesus Christ, are known by God, and are no longer under bondage, Paul asks why they would go back into bondage? Why would they go back into the weak and beggarly (4434:ptochos:*pto-khos'*:**used as an adjective describing one who crouches and cowers; poverty-stricken, powerless to enrich, metaphorically [metaphorically – *a figure of speech, figurative speech*] descriptive of the religion of the Jews**), worthless things to become slaves to these things again? Christ has set us free from religious "gobbledygook." Paul is trying to get them to think about what they are doing and see the big picture. This question still applies and is apropos to Christians today. Many Christians are still bound by man-made religious practices such as prohibiting wearing makeup and strict worship service attendance rules, even though Christ has set us free.

The Judaizers enticed these Galatian Christians to go back into ritualistic practices and ceremonial Laws. They were told to observe certain days, special weeks / months, and seasons. This proves they submitted themselves under the law of Moses. Paul was very concerned; he was afraid that his labor was in vain. Paul pleaded with them to be like he is, free from the bondage of Jewish ritualism, legalistic practices, and ordinances. Paul was raised in the bondage of the Jewish religion and he became free through faith in the gospel of Jesus Christ. Paul reminds them that they did not harm him (being a Jew) when he first witnessed to them; likewise, he pleads with them not to harm or hurt him now by going into the ritualism of the law of Moses.

Has the Galatian Christians' Love for Paul and His Ministry Grown Cold?

vv. 13-16   Paul leaves no stone unturned in dealing with the Galatian Christians. Christians – especially ministers of the gospel of Christ – should take this principle to heart when dealing with people who deviate from the truth of the gospel of Christ. Ephesians 4:27 tells us not to give the enemy (Satan) any place. This means don't give the enemy any room to operate.

Paul brings up another point. He reminds the Galatian Christians that while he was in Galatia, he had a bodily injury or infirmity (weakness) in his flesh. This might've been offensive to the Galatians. The Amplified Bible explains that Paul's bodily ailment actually caused him to remain in Galatia and preach the gospel of Jesus Christ to them. Infirmity or not, the Galatians received Paul and his ministry with joy and gladness. They did not despise or reject Paul, but received him as though he was an angel or Christ Himself. They received Paul with joy, affection, regard, and confidence. Paul asks them where is that great joy, affection, regard and confidence now? What happened to that blessedness and enjoyment they had when they received the preaching of the gospel of Jesus Christ? They were so glad when they received the gospel from Paul that they would have taken out their own eyes and given them to Paul if it would have promoted his comfort and welfare.

Note: Some scholars say that Paul's infirmity was blindness. They get this from the reference of "eyes" in verse 15. I have heard arguments on both sides. Paul did have an infirmity in his flesh; however, I don't necessarily believe that it was his eyes, because I don't know of any other Biblical reference to this belief.

Paul doesn't seem to get the same joyful reception now. He asks if he had become their enemy because he spoke the truth to them. What we can gather from this is that not everyone is going to be happy when the truth is proclaimed. Christians (especially ministers of the gospel of Jesus Christ) must learn how to stand with the truth and proclaim it no matter what. Integrity must be maintained at all cost. When you stand for the truth, you will make some enemies. Today, they will say Hosanna! Tomorrow, they will say crucify him!

Tactics of the Judaizing Teachers

vv. 17-20   The Judaizers were very interested in the Galatians. They took great effort in trying to dazzle and zealously affect them pretty much in the same way a man shows interest in a woman he is courting with less than honorable intentions. The Galatians enjoyed receiving all this attention from the Judaizers, but Paul exposed their motives. Paul tells them that the Judaizers' purpose is not honorable, worthy, nor good in any way. He tells them that the Judaziers want to isolate them from the teachings of Paul so that they may win them over to their side where they practice the law of Moses. Paul also tells them that, although it is a good thing to be zealously sought after and affected as they were, it must be for a good purpose, not with clandestine motives. The enemy always comes to us with an appealing appearance and good words and deeds. Ungodly motives and purposes are always cloaked, revealing their true motives a little bit over time. We must be aware of this common tactic of the enemy. God never hides anything from us.

The Spirit of God is always up front, honest, and gives total disclosure.

Paul affectionately referred to the Galatian Christians as "little children." Paul must have felt like a parent to them. Paul feels as though he is suffering birth pangs again until Christ is completely and permanently formed (3445:morphoo:*mor-fo'-o*:**to fashion; refers not to the external or transient, but to the inward and real; used in this Scripture expressing the necessity of a change in character and conduct to correspond with inward spiritual condition**) in them. The revelation here is that when a person accepts Jesus Christ as their Savior and Lord, speaking metaphorically, it is like at the point of physical conception: The seed, the Spirit of Christ, is planted in us by the Holy Spirit, however the seed (metaphorically) does form into a human body. We permit the seed of the Spirit of Christ to form in us, and in this case, there is no possibility of abortion. Outside influences can have an affect on the growth of a fetus such as drugs, alcohol, lack of nourishment. These outside influences can have lasting effects on the child for many years. The same can be true for a person that has just been born again. In the tender state of being a baby Christian, outside influences such as fanatics, wrong friends and a lack of sound teaching can have a lasting negative affect on the growth of a baby Christian. They can grow with a warped and distorted view of God and have a strange and unhealthy fellowship with the Father. Paul is fearful and perplexed about the Galatian Christians. He wants to be with them at this time

so he himself can persuade and coax them directly.
At present, He is not sure of their outcome.

Paul's Allegory of Sarah and Hagar (Faith and the Law)

vv. 21-26   Paul addresses people who choose to be under
the law of Moses. In his effort to persuade them
away from the law of Moses, he asked them if they
can hear what the Law is really saying. He paints
an allegory using Sarah, Abraham's wife, and
Hagar, Sarah's servant (bondmaid), who each had
a son from Abraham. The child born of the servant
woman was born according to the flesh (according
the law of natural generation), an ordinary birth.
The son born of the free woman was born in fulfill-
ment of a promise (by the supernatural power of
God). These two women represent the two cove-
nants. One covenant (Hagar's) came from Mount
Sinai, where the law of Moses was given, and
produces children destined for bondage. Paul says
that Hagar represents Mount Sinai in Arabia. She,
along with her children, belongs in the category of
the current Jerusalem. She is in bondage. The other
covenant (Sarah's) came from the Jerusalem from
above – the Messianic kingdom of Christ – and is
free from bondage. All Believers are recipients of
this covenant.

v. 27   This verse seems a little hard to understand
without explanation. Paul is referencing Isaiah
54:1. This is a prophecy about when the Gentiles
will accept the gospel of Jesus Christ – the Christian

dispensation. The Gentiles were barren and desolate until Christ came. The Jews had God as their husband. Rejoice! For Christ has come.

vv. 28-31   Paul tells the Galatian Christians that we're brothers and are as Isaac was – children of the promise, not according to physical descent, as was Ishmael, but as Isaac, born of the Spirit in virtue of promise.

Just like Ishmael, who was born of ordinary birth, despised and persecuted Isaac who was born of a remarkable birth, of the promise and working of the Holy Spirit. The hatred and persecution is the same today. Those that choose to follow the law of Moses for their justification, despise and persecute those that choose to accept the gospel of Jesus Christ by faith as their justification. This existed not only in Paul's time, but also exists today. Carnal Christians are opposed to Spirit-filled Christians today. This division in the body of Christ started back then in Paul's time and the division has grown and is alive and well today in the body of Christ. Today, the body of Christ has countless many divisions. This was never Christ's vision for the body of Christ, the church.

Scripture tells us to cast out the bondwoman and her son! In other words, just like the bondwoman (Hagar) and her son (Ishmael) were cast out of the camp, so all ceremonial observances and the legalistic practices of the law of Moses should be excluded from Christianity as a requirement for justification. All who seek salvation and justification by works of the law of Moses, or any other more contemporary works, will utterly fail. Why cast them out? Why can't we coexist together? The reason is simple. The son of the bondwoman will not be heir and will not share the inheritance with the son of the freewoman (Genesis 21:10). We're not children of the bondwoman – the law of Moses and its rituals, ceremony and legalistic practices – but we're children of the freewoman – the promise of the gospel of Jesus Christ through faith.

Summary and Conclusion

We're not merely just servants of God, but we're sons and daughters of God. As such, we enjoy a closer fellowship with our Father, God, as well as a Father and child relationship with God. The question is, *why would anyone want to go back into servitude after enjoying the benefits of the sonship in Christ?* In servitude, there is bondage. In sonship, there is freedom. Paul wondered whether he had become their enemy because he told them the truth. When you stand for truth, someone is not going to like it. These Judaizers were like wolves in sheep's clothing. They showed honest interest in the Galatian Christians, but their motive was to isolate them from Paul's teachings and pull them into the bondage of the Law. Baby Christians must be protected until Christ is "formed" in them. Paul concluded that we're not children of the bondwoman (Hagar) – the law of Moses, but we're children of the freewoman (Sarah) – the gospel of Jesus Christ through faith.

Personal Notes

CHAPTER 5

Call to Freedom and Liberty from the Bondage of the Law

vv. 1 – 12   Paul summarizes his argument and repositions his focus and encourages the Galatian Christians to stand and maintain their freedom and liberty that Christ has made available to them. He advises them not to submit to the bondage of the law of Moses. In today's society, there are still strategies and things that can put Christians in bondage: legalistic practices, rituals, by-laws, financial pressures, sicknesses, prejudices, fear, phobias, obesity, and so forth. Because Christ has set us free, we're encouraged to stand in the liberty Christ has made available to us.

Some go the way of circumcision and submit themselves to the law of Moses in order to gain salvation and justification. The law of Moses was never given for salvation and justification (Galatians 3:21). Those who depend upon the law of Moses for salvation don't believe that Christ's work is sufficient to redeem and justify humankind. Paul reminds them again that to receive circumcision places them under the law of Moses, and that they must keep the *whole* Law or else the curse of the Law will overtake them (Galatians 3:10). Accepting the way of the law of Moses separates one from Christ and redemption; they are outside of the grace of God that He provided in Jesus Christ. People who try to be justified by the law of Moses reject the redemptive work of Christ. There is no salvation, justification, or righteousness without Christ.

The true Believers wait for the hope of salvation, justification, and righteousness through faith, and God bestows the Holy Spirit upon those who believe on His Son (Romans 1:17). Keeping and following the Law doesn't have anything to do with salvation in Christ. By God's grace, we receive salvation through faith – based in love – in the gospel of Jesus Christ.

When the Galatians first received the teachings of Paul, the gospel of Jesus Christ, they believed, received, and followed without error. They started out well. Paul asked them the rhetorical question, "Who did hinder you that ye should now not obey the truth?" Paul was saying that he had given them the truth of the gospel of Jesus Christ and now they are listening and following the teachings of someone (the Judaizers) who has given them something other than the truth. They told them things such as, it was needful to be circumcised and observe Jewish rites to obtain salvation, but this is incorrect for a requirement of salvation. Paul states in verse 9, "A little leaven leaveneth the whole lump." This means that a little error introduced by false teachers will vitiate (vitiate – *to impair the value or quality of; make faulty or impure; spoil; to corrupt morally; pervert; to invalidate or render legally ineffective*) the whole body of Christians, unless it is abandoned.

Paul – through the Lord – had a hope and strong confidence that they would reflect on what he has said and get back on the right track and abandon the teachings of the Judaizers. The false teachers who created this unrest among the Galatian Christians will bear the judgment due them.

Paul reiterates again to the Galatian Christians that if he subscribed to circumcision and the doctrine of justification through keeping and doing the ritual practices of the law of Moses, then why is he persecuted? There would be no reason. The stumbling block and offence of the cross would be done away with. Paul's desire was that the Judaizing teachers would just go away and be cut off (609:apokopto: *ap-ok-op'-to*:**to amputate; excommunicate**).

Christian Liberty and Freedom with Boundaries

vv. 13-18   Paul wants the Galatian Christians to know that with their new found freedom and liberty there is responsibility and boundaries. We're free from the ritual practices and legalisms of the law of Moses and we're free from the curse of the Law altogether. In experiencing this new freedom, he encourages Believers not to use it for a license to indulge the sins and selfishness of the flesh. But through love we're to serve each other. The law of Moses is fulfilled in love; that we love each other (our neighbors) as we love ourselves.

Paul also gives a warning: If we bite and devour each other with negative words and harmful deeds, then our fellowship will be consumed by each other. We're to live our lives loving each other. If you love me, you will do me no harm.

We live our lives according to our newly regenerated spirits, influenced by the Spirit of Christ residing in us. In doing so, we will *not* fulfill the lust for sinful acts that is in our flesh, which comes to our flesh through our senses. It is interesting to note that even though we have the Spirit of Christ in us and the spirit of man has been regenerated (becoming a new creature), our body still lusts after and longs for the sinful acts of the flesh. It comes down to a choice: listen and submit to the Spirit of Christ or listen and submit to the lust in our flesh. We get to choose.

The newly regenerated spirit will always oppose the lust and desires of the senses – the flesh. The flesh and the spirit always pull in opposite directions, antagonizing each other. Those who are led by their regenerated spirit are not under the law of Moses, but under the law of Love. The law of Moses dealt with the children of Israel through the senses of the flesh. Even though they practiced the rituals of the law of Moses, their heart (for the most part) was not involved. They followed the law of Moses with their flesh (senses) and not necessarily their heart. They observed and performed the legalistic practices of the law of Moses because they knew they were supposed to, not because they wanted to. To say it bluntly, they kept the law of Moses, not to please God out of a heart of love, but to keep God off their backs.

Acts That Satisfy the Senses

vv. 19-21   Paul catalogues some of the main acts of the corruption of human nature not controlled by the regenerated human spirit. Acts that satisfy the flesh are as follows:

1. Adultery   (3430:mŏichĕia: *moy-khi'-ah*: **adultery; one who has unlawful intercourse with the spouse of another**).

2. Fornication   (4202:pŏrnĕia:*por-ni'-ah*: **harlotry; illicit [illicit – *not sanctioned by custom or law; illegal; unlawful*] sexual intercourse**).

3. Uncleanness   (167:akatharsia: *ak-ath-ar-see'-ah*: **impurity; uncleanness, physical or moral; suggestive of**

the fact that sensuality [sensuality *– pertaining to or given to the gratification of the physical appetites, especially sexual appetites]* **and evil doctrine are frequently associated).** In the context of this Scripture, the emphasis is on moral impurity rather than physical impurity.

4. Lasciviousness

(766:asĕlgĕia:*as-elg'-i-a***: filthy; denotes excess, licentiousness [licentiousness** *– lacking moral discipline or sexual restraint. Having no regard for accepted rules or standards]*, **absence of restraint, indecency, wantonness [wantonness –** *immoral or unchaste; lewd. Maliciously cruel; merciless; unjust. Freely extravagant; excessive. An immoral, lewd, or*

licentious person,
especially a woman.])

5. Idolatry

(1495:ĕidōlŏlatrĕia:
i-do-lol-at-ri'-ah:
image-worship)

6. Witchcraft

(5331:pharmakĕia:
far-mak-i'-ah: **magic;**
sorcery [sorcery
– the use of super-
natural power over
others through the
assistance of evil
spirits]; **medicine,**
durgs, spells, then
poisoning, then
sorcery).

7. Hatred

(2189:ĕchthra:*ekh'-*
thrah: **hostility;**
enmity;)

8. Variance

(2054:ĕris:*er'-is*:
a quarrel; wran-
gling [wrangling
– to dispute noisily
or angrily; bicker],
contention, debate,
strife [strife *– heated,*
often violent
display of a differ-

*ence of opinion
{dissension}*])

9. Emulation

(2205:zēlŏs:*dzay'-los*:
**jealousy; zeal; envy;
effort or ambition
to equal or surpass
another when moti-
vated by jealousy
and envy**)

10. Wrath

(2372:thumŏs:*thoo-
mos'*: **passion; fierce-
ness; indignation;
hot anger; when
smoldering in the
heart, break out
with wrath**)

11. Strife

(2052: ĕrithĕia:
er-ith-i'-ah: **conten-
tion; denotes ambi-
tion, self seeking,
rivalry [rivalry –** *the
act of competing
or emulating; the
state or condition of
being a rival*]**; party-
making; faction
[faction –** *a group
of persons forming
a cohesive, usually
contentious, minority*

within a larger group; internal dissension]; **seeking to win followers**)

12. Sedition

(1370:dichŏstasia: *dee-khos-tas-ee'-ah*: **disunion; division; sedition [sedition –** *conduct or language inciting to rebellion against the authority of the state*]; **a standing apart**)

13. Heresy

(139:hairĕsis:*hah'ee-res-is*: **a choice; a party; disunion; that which is chosen, and hence, an opinion, especially a self-willed opinion, which is substituted for submission to the power of truth, and leads to division and the formation of sects**)

14. Envy

(5355:phthŏnŏs: *fthon'-os*: **ill-will; jealousy; is the feeling of displea-**

**sure produced
by witnessing or
hearing of the
advantage or pros-
perity of others)**

15. Murder

(5408:phŏnŏs:*fon'-os*:
**to slay; be slain with,
slaughter)**

16. Drunkenness

(3178:mĕthĕ:*meth'-
ay*: **habitual intoxica-
tion; strong drink)**

17. Reveling

(2970:kōmŏs:*ko'-
mos*: **a carousal
[carousal –** *a jovial,
riotous drinking
party; boisterous
merrymaking;
revelry*]; **as if a
letting loose; rioting)**

Paul warns the Galatian Christians that those who choose to participate in such acts (and additional behaviors such as these) will not inherit the kingdom of God. In other words, they might be born again (however, it is most likely such people are not born of the Spirit to begin with), but they will not share in the benefits of the kingdom of God.

The Fruit of the Recreated Human Spirit

vv. 22-23   In contrast, Paul catalogues the fruits of the Spirit – the demonstrated characteristics of the Believer's life controlled by the regenerated human spirit:

1. Love

(26:agapē:*ag-ah'-pay*: **affection; benevolence; love feast; in this setting, it is used to convey His will to His children concerning their attitude one toward another. Love can be known only its actions. Obviously, this is not the love of complacency or affection; it is not drawn out by any excellency in its object)**

2. Joy

(5479:chara:*khar-ah'*: **cheerfulness; calm delight; gladness; to rejoice)**

3. Peace

(1515:ĕirēnē:*i-ray'-nay*: **one; quietness;**

**rest; harmony;
friendliness)**

4. Longsuffering

(3115:makrŏthumia:
mak-roth-oo-mee'-ah:
**longanimity [longa-
nimity –** *equanimity
{equanimity – the
quality or character-
istic of being calm
and even-tempered;
composure, especially
in the face of trying
circumstances} in the
face of suffering and
adversity]*; **forbear-
ance; fortitude;
patience)**

5. Gentleness

Translated "kindness"
(5544:chrēstŏtēs:
khray-stol'-ace:
**goodness; kindness;
serviceable, good,
pleasant, gracious)**

6. Goodness

(19:agathōsunē:
ag-ath-o-soo'-nay:
**virtune or benefi-
cence [beneficence**
*– the quality of
charity or kind-
ness]*; **signifies a**

moral quality that is described as being morally honorable and pleasing to God and beneficial; of regenerate persons)

7. Faith (4102:pistis:*pis'-tis*: assurance, belief, fidelity; firm persuasion; conviction based upon hearing [R.V., "faithfulness"])

8. Meekness (4236:praiŏtēs: *prah-ot'-ace*: gentleness; mild; not an outward behavior only, rather it is an inwrought grace of the soul. It does not struggle or fight against God; does not imply weakness or spinelessness)

9. Temperance (1466:ĕgkratĕia: *eng-krat'-i-ah*: self-control; strength; the controlling power of the will

**under the operation
of the Spirit of God)**

As the Holy Spirit leads our recreated spirit, we mature and manifest this fruit, of our recreated spirit, in our everyday lives. No law can stand against this fruit and bring a charge against us.

vv. 24-26   Paul explains that those who belong to Christ are to crucify or mortify their flesh along with its passions, appetites and desires. It is our responsibility to crucify the flesh. God doesn't do it for us but He does helps us. The power of the Holy Spirit gives us the strength to crucify the flesh.

Because we live (2198:zaō:*dzah'-o*:**to live; life, quick; be alive**) and have life (*inner life*) in the recreated human spirit, we ought to walk (4748: stŏichĕō:*stoy-kheh'-o*:**to march in military rank; keep step; to conform to virtue and piety [piety – devotion and reverence to God]**) and follow the leading of our recreated spirit in our outward life. Our outward conduct is to be governed by the recreated human spirit, which is influenced by the Spirit of Christ in us. We're not to seek vain glory (2755:kenodoxos:*ken-od'-ox-os*:**vainly glorifying; boastful; self-conceited; empty glory**) and be conceited. We're not to be boastful, provoke, challenge, and irritate each other. We're not to be envious and jealous of each other.

Summary and Conclusion

We have been freed from the bondage of the legalisms, ritualistic practices, and observances of the law of Moses. We're not to abuse our liberty and use it to deliberately commit sinful acts. We're justified only because of God's grace through faith in the shed blood of Jesus Christ. There is no justification in circumcision nor in any part of the law of Moses. Only the law of love binds us. We're to love each other. We're to live our lives by manifesting the fruit of our recreated spirit and follow the leading of our spirit influenced by the Spirit of Christ in us, and not follow the lust of the flesh. We're to crucify the flesh and allow the fruit of our recreated spirit to grow in us and manifest in our lives as we interact with our fellow Christians and others.

Personal Notes

_____

_____

_____

_____

_____

_____

_____

_____

_____

_____

_____

_____

_____

_____

_____

_____

_____

_____

_____

_____

CHAPTER 6

Christian Duty and Responsibility

vv. 1-10   Paul closes his epistle to the Galatian Christians by touching on the following several points of Christian responsibility. Love is the motivation in performing our Christian duty.

    A. Paul instructs the Galatian Christians about their attitude when it comes to correcting a person overtaken in misconduct or sin. He says those who are spiritual (*who are responsive to and controlled by their recreated spirit and those who are under the influence of the indwelling Spirit of Christ and advanced in Christian knowledge, experience and wisdom*) are to set the offending person right and give the individual an opportunity to repent. Secondly, our goal should be toward restoration and reinstatement. Restore that person in meekness and gentleness, not arrogantly or with a sense of superiority. In addition, we're to keep a close eye on our own attitude to make sure we're not given over to the temptation of looking down on the offending person with our wrong attitude.

B. Another Christian duty is that we ought to endure and carry each other's burdens (922: barŏs:*bar'-os*: **weight, load; a demand on one's resources**).

Note: In this setting, the word "burden" refers more toward spiritual or emotional burdens (i.e., moral faults, etc.) rather than physical or financial burdens.

A fellow Christian struggling with troublesome moral faults shouldn't feel like they're isolated and alone. We should be there for them and help them along the right path, not with an attitude of judgment but an attitude of prayer, love, and genuine concern. By doing this, we fulfill the law of Christ – the law of love. If a person thinks they're too important (*has an exalted opinion of ones knowledge and attainments as a Christian; false pride*) to condescend to shoulder another's load, that person is deceived and cheats them self. Paul instructs us to carefully examine and scrutinize our conduct and work. Then, we can have the personal satisfaction (*the joy of doing something commendable*), without resorting to boastful comparisons, "showing off" to our neighbors, and looking to fellow Christians for praise and accolades. Everyone will have to shoulder (*bear*), understand, and calmly receive their own load of oppressive moral faults. We can share and sympathize (even empathize) with our fellow Christians, but not necessarily share their responsibility.

C. Paul makes another important point here. Those who are taught and receive instruction from the Word of God should contribute (*give*) to the support of the teacher. God is not mocked, meaning He does not allow people to trifle with Him or His requirements. You will reap what you sow. A person that sows to the flesh (indulges their fleshly passions and appetites) will reap the ruin and bodily corruption as their outcome. The person that sows to the Spirit (yielding their life to God's guidance and control) and allows the fruit of their recreated human spirit to grow in them, will reap in due season life everlasting. Paul also warns against becoming weary in doing good deeds. We will reap in due season, if we don't quit. As opportunities present themselves, we should do good toward all humankind, especially to those of like precious faith.

Summary of the Doctrine of the Judaizers

vv. 11-18   Paul is closing his epistle to the Galatian Christians. He tells them to be aware of how large of a letter he has written to them by his own hand and to pay close attention to his closing words.

The Judaizer's basic motive was to make a good showing or impression of outward ceremonies so they can be esteemed among carnal people (people governed by the flesh) by compelling the Galatian Christians to receive circumcision and observe the law of Moses to avoid Jewish persecution. Otherwise, they would have been accused of an allegiance to the gospel of Christ; justification by God's grace through faith in the shed blood of Jesus Christ. The Jews themselves didn't really keep the entire law of Moses, but they wanted the Galatian Christians to receive circumcision and follow the law of Moses (to join their party) so they could boast in the Galatian Christian's subjection to their external rites, their flesh. Paul said, far be it from him that he should boast in anyone or anything except in the cross of the Lord Jesus Christ. Through the cross of Christ, the world (2889:kŏsmŏs:*kos'-mos*:**orderly arrangement; decoration; adorning; in this case, it is used to denote the present condition of human affairs, in alienation from the opposition of God**) is crucified to the Christian and the Christian is crucified to the world.

Both circumcision and uncircumcision have no importance, meaning or significance. The only thing that is important, has meaning, and is very significant is our new creation, our new nature in Jesus Christ that is the result of the new birth. Paul gives his benediction and grants God's peace and mercy be upon all (the true Israel of God) who live their lives by the rule of love and embrace salvation by God's grace through faith in the shed blood of Jesus Christ.

Paul ends his epistle to the Galatian Christians by requesting that from now on, he be not troubled and made to vindicate and defend his apostolic authority and the truth of the gospel, because he bears on his body the marks of the Lord Jesus Christ – the wounds, scars, and other outward evidence of persecution. Paul desired that the grace of the Lord Jesus Christ be with their spirit. Ā-měn´.

Summary and Conclusion

As we perform our Christian duty and responsibility, we're to be motivated by love. We're to allow the fruit of our recreated human spirit to mature in us and manifest in our everyday lives; love is to be our motivation. Christians are to allow the love of Christ to mature in their lives. The Judaizers were motivated by fear, wanting to control the Galatian Christians. The Judaizing teachers wanted to put the Galatian Christians in bondage under the legalistic practices and rituals of the law of Moses. They themselves didn't really follow the entire law of Moses. They wanted to make a good showing to their peers for fear of being considered having an allegiance to the gospel of Christ. Circumcision nor uncircumcision have any importance. What is important is a new creation that is the result of the new birth and a new nature in Jesus Christ.

Personal Notes

Glossary

Accursed	7045:*qelalah*: **curse; vilification [vilification** – *defame, denigrate*]**; execration [(execrate** – *to inveigh) (*inveigh – *to give vent to angry censure; protest with intense emotion or conviction)*]** against; denounce.**
Admonish	**To reprove mildly or kindly, but seriously.**
Adultery	3430:mŏichĕia:*moy-khi'-ah*: **adultery; one who has unlawful intercourse with the spouse of another**.
Age	165:aion:*ahee-ohn'*: **a period of indefinite duration. Not so much the length of a period, but a period marked by spiritual or moral characteristics.**
Angel	32:aggelos:*ang'-el*-os: **a messenger sent whether by God, man, or Satan.**

Apostle

652:apostolos:*ap-os'-tol-os*: **one sent forth.**

Beggarly

4434:ptochos:*pto-khos'*: **used as an adjective describing one who crouches and cowers; poverty-stricken; powerless to enrich; metaphorically descriptive of the religion of the Jews.**

Bewitched

940:baskaino:*bas-kah'-ee-no*: **fascinate by false representation; to mislead by an evil eye; to charm; leading into evil doctrine.**

Burdens

922:barŏs:*bar'-os*: **weight; load; a demand on one's resources.**

Certify

1107:gnorizo:*gno-rid'-zo*: **to make known; declare; give to understand.**

Conversation

391:anastrophe:*an-as-trof-ay'*: **behavior; manner of life.**

Curse

2671:katara:*kat-ar'-ah*: **denotes an execration [(execrate –** *to inveigh)* **(inveigh –** *to give vent to angry censure; protest with intense emotion or conviction)*] **against; denounce; imprecation [imprecation –** *to invoke (evil or a curse) upon*]; **curse, uttered out of malevolence [malevolence –** *ill will toward others; wishing harm to others*]

Cursed	331:anathema:*an-ath'-em-ah*: **excommunicated; the disfavor of Jehovah; devoted to destruction; doomed to eternal punishment.**
Cut off	609:apokopto:*ap-ok-op'-to*: **to amputate; excommunicate.**
Disannul	208:akuroo:ak-oo-ro'-o: to invalidate; to make ineffective; to make void; to deprive of authority.
Dissimulation	5272:hupokrisis:*hoop-ok'-ree-sis*: **acting under a feigned [feign – *to give a false appearance, not real, pretend*] part; deceit.**
Drunkenness	3178:mĕthĕ:*meth'-ay*: **habitual intoxication; strong drink.**
Emulation	2205:zēlŏs:*dzay'-los*: **jealousy; zeal; envy; effort or ambition to equal or surpass another when motivated by jealousy and envy.**
Envy	5355:phthŏnŏs:*fthon'-os*: **ill will; jealousy; the feeling of displeasure produced by witnessing or hearing of the advantage or prosperity of others.**
Epistle	**A formal written letter.**

Faith

4102:pistis:*pis'-tis*: **assurance; belief; fidelity; firm persuasion; conviction based upon hearing [R.V., "faithfulness"].**

Foolish

453:anoetos:*an-o'-ay-tos*: **unintelligent; unwise; signifies not understanding, an unworthy lack of understanding; senseless.**

Formed

3445:morphoo:*mor-fo'-o*: **to fashion; refers not to the external or transient, but to the inward and real; used in this Scripture expressing the necessity of a change in character and conduct to correspond with inward spiritual condition.**

Fornication

4202:pŏrnĕia:*por-ni'-ah*: **harlotry; illicit [illicit – *not sanctioned by custom or law; illegal; unlawful*] sexual intercourse.**

Frustrate

114:atheteo:*ath-et-eh'-o*: **to set aside, disesteem, neutralize, or violate; to make void.**

Gentleness

This word should be translated "kindness" (5544:chrēstŏtēs:*khray-stol'-ace*: **goodness; kindness; serviceable; good; pleasant; gracious**).

Glory	**The physical manifestation of the power of God.**
Goodness	19:agathōsunē:*ag-ath-o-soo'-nay*: **virtue or beneficence [beneficence** *– the quality of charity or kindness*]; **signifies a moral quality that is morally honorable, pleasing to God, and beneficial; of regenerate persons.**
Gospel	2098:euaggelion:*yoo-ang-ghel'-ee-on*: **the good news or good tidings of the kingdom of God.**
Grace	5485:charis:*khar'-ece*: **favor.**
Hatred	2189:ĕchthra:*ekh'-thrah*: **hostility; enmity.**
Heresies	139:hairĕsis:*hah'ee-res-is*: **a choice; a party; disunion; that which is chosen, and hence, an opinion, especially a self-willed opinion, which is substituted for submission to the power of truth, and leads to division and the formation of sects.**
Idolatry	1495:ĕidōlŏlatrĕia:*i-do-lol-at-ri'-ah*: **image worship.**
Joy	5479:chara:*khar-ah'*: **cheerfulness; calm delight; gladness; to rejoice.**

Judaizers	**Jews who believed that total salvation was not just by faith; that one must also be circumcised and observe the legalistic practices, traditions, and rituals of the law of Moses. (Some professed to be Christians and some only acknowledged Jesus as Messiah.)**
Lasciviousness	766:asĕlgĕia:*as-elg'-i-a*: **filthy; denotes excess; licentiousness [licentious-ness –** *lacking moral discipline or sexual restraint. Having no regard for accepted rules or standards]*, **absence of restraint; indecency; wantonness [wantonness –** *immoral or unchaste; lewd. Maliciously cruel; merciless; unjust. Freely extravagant; excessive. An immoral, lewd, or licentious person, especially a woman.]*
Life	2198:zao:*dzah'-o*: **to live, be alive; spiritual life.**
Live	2198:zaō:*dzah'-o*: **to live; life, quick; be alive.**
Longsuffering	3115:makrŏthumia:*mak-roth-oo-mee'-ah*: **longanimity [longanimity –** *equanimity {equanimity – the quality or characteristic of being calm and even-tempered; composure, especially in the face of trying circumstances}* **in**

96

the face of suffering and adversity];
forbearance; fortitude; patience.

Love   26:agapē:*ag-ah'-pay*: **affection; benevolence; love feast; in this setting, it is
used to convey His will to His children
concerning their attitude one toward
another. Love can be known only by
its actions. Obviously this is not the
love of complacency or affection; it is
not drawn out by any excellency in its
object.**

Magna Carta   **A document that serves as a guarantee
of basic rights.**

Meekness   4236:praiŏtēs:*prah-ot'-ace*: **gentleness;
mild; not just an outward behavior
but an inwrought grace of the soul.
It does not struggle or fight against
God;** *does not imply weakness or
spinelessness.*

Miracles   1411:dunamis:*doo'-nam-is*: **power,
inherent ability; works of a super-
natural origin and character; cannot
be produced by natural agents and
means.**

Murders   5408:phŏnŏs:*fon'-os*: **to slay; be slain
with, slaughter.**

Paul   3972:Paulos:*pow'-los*.

Peace	1515:ĕirēnē:*i-ray'-nay*: **one; quietness; rest; harmony; friendliness.**
Persecuted	1377:dioko:*dee-o'-ko*: **to put to flight, drive away; press toward.**
Persuade	3982:peitho:*pi'-tho*: **to apply persuasion; to prevail upon or win over; to persuade; bringing about a change of mind by the influence of reason or moral considerations.**
Perverted	3344:metastrepho:*met-as-tref'-o*: **to transform into something of an opposite character.**
Pleased	2106:eudokeo:*yoo-dok-eh'*: **to be well pleased; think it good; not merely an understanding of what is right and good, but stressing the willingness and freedom of an intention or resolve regarding what is good.**
Profited	4298:prokopto:*prok-op'-to*: **to drive forward, advance; to grow, increase.**
Repute	1380:dokeo:*dok-eh'-o*:**well thought of; which were of reputation.**
Reveling	2970:kōmŏs:*ko'-mos*: **a carousal** [carousal – *a jovial, riotous drinking party; boisterous merrymaking; revelry*]; **as if a letting loose; rioting.**

Sedition	1370:dichŏstasia:*dee-khos-tas-ee'-ah*: disunion; division; sedition [sedition – *conduct or language inciting to rebellion against the authority of the state*]; a standing apart.
Servant	1401:dŏulŏs:*doo'-los*: frequently indicating subjection without the idea of bondage; used metaphorically of spiritual, moral and ethical conditions.
Suffered	3958:pascho:*pas'-kho*: to experience a sensation or impression, usually painful.
Strife	2052: ĕrithĕia:*er-ith-i'-ah*: contention; denotes ambition, self seeking, rivalry [rivalry – *the act of competing or emulating; the state or condition of being a rival*]; party-making; faction [faction – *a group of persons forming a cohesive, usually contentious, minority within a larger group; internal dissension*]; seeking to win followers.
Temperance	1466:ĕgkratĕia:*eng-krat'-i-ah*: self-control; strength; the controlling power of the will under the operation of the Spirit of God.
Transgressions	3847:parabasis:*par-ab'-as-is*: violation, breaking; is used metaphorically

to denote transgression ; always of a
breach of law.

Uncleanness

167:akatharsia:*ak-ath-ar-see'-ah*: **impurity; uncleanness, physical or moral;
suggestive of the fact that sensuality**
[**sensuality** – *pertaining to or given to
the gratification of the physical appetites, especially sexual appetites*] **and
evil doctrine are frequently associated**). In the context of this Scripture,
the emphasis is on moral impurity rather
than physical impurity..

Vain glory

2755:kenodoxos:*ken-od'-ox-os*: **vainly
glorifying; boastful; self-conceited;
empty glory.**

Variance

2054:ĕris:*er'-is*: **a quarrel; wrangling**
[**wrangling** – *to dispute noisily or
angrily; bicker*], **contention, debate,
strife** [**strife** – *heated, often violent
display of a difference of opinion
{dissension}*].

Vitiate

To impair the value or quality of; make
faulty or impure; spoil; to corrupt
morally; pervert; to invalidate or render
legally ineffective.

Walk

4748:stŏichĕō:*stoy-kheh'-o*: **to march in
military rank; keep step; to conform**

to virtue and piety [piety – devotion and reverence to God.]

Wasted

4199:portheo:*por-theh'-o* :**to ravage; destroy; waste.**

Witchcraft

5331:pharmakĕia:*far-mak-i'-ah*: **magic; sorcery** [sorcery – *the use of supernatural power over others through the assistance of evil spirits*]; **medicine; drugs; spells; poisoning; sorcery.**

World

2889:kŏsmŏs:*kos'-mos*: **orderly arrangement; decoration; adorning; in this case, it is used to denote the present condition of human affairs in alienation from the opposition of God.**

Wrath

2372:thumŏs:*thoo-mos'*: **passion; fierceness; indignation; hot anger; when smoldering in the heart; break out with wrath.**

Personal Notes

Personal Notes

Personal Notes

Personal Notes

Personal Notes

Personal Notes

CPSIA information can be obtained at www.ICGtesting.com
Printed in the USA
LVOW091933040612

284612LV00001B/409/A